ARCTIC HEART

Other Books by Gretel Ehrlich

GEODE ROCK BODY *(poems)*

TO TOUCH THE WATER *(poems)*

THE SOLACE OF OPEN SPACES *(essays)*

HEART MOUNTAIN *(novel)*

DRINKING DRY CLOUDS *(stories)*

ISLANDS, THE UNIVERSE, HOME *(essays)*

ARCTIC HEART

A POEM CYCLE
GRETEL EHRLICH

IMAGERY
DAVID BUCKLAND

CAPRA PRESS
SANTA BARBARA

LIBRARY OF CONGRESS CATALOGING-IN-PUBLICATION DATA

Ehrlich, Gretel.
Arctic heart : a poem cycle / Gretel Ehrlich:
imagery by David Buckland
p.   cm.
ISBN 0-88496-357-8 (pbk.) : $14.95
1. Arctic regions—Poetry. I. Title.
PS3555.H72A7   1992   92-15095
811'.54—dc20   CIP

CAPRA PRESS

P.O. Box 2068
Santa Barbara, CA 93120

WITH SPECIAL THANKS TO THE

Siobhan Davies Dance Company
&
Brendan Kelly

FOREWORD

This poem cycle was written in London during the summer of 1991 after a visit to the Canadian High Arctic in May. I had been invited there by a friend and biologist, Brendan Kelly, who studies the evolutionary history of Arctic seals, and was later commissioned by *Harper's* magazine to write about ephemeral landscape. We lived in a tent on frozen seas under continuous sun. Our in-tent music was the sound of seals breathing, amplified by hydrophones lowered down into their lairs. We live-captured seals with Brendan's ingeniously designed nets, tagged and released them, followed their movements and dives on computer screens. A fierce arctic storm engulfed us, buried our food cache and snowmobiles; wind dismantled the tents, then left us in the embrace of balmy arctic warmth that cracked the ice floor.

From Resolute, N.W.T. I flew to London where I had been asked by the choreographer, Siobhan Davies, to write a text to accompany a new ballet. We had never met or discussed how we would work together. On arrival I was taken directly to the rehearsal studio in Soho. After introductions to her six dancers, David Buckland the set designer, and Jean Marc the composer, I fell asleep on the floor.

But the next morning I began writing in my quiet London flat lent to me by a friend. While Siobhan had expected words about Wyoming, what came out were these poems about the Arctic. My daily routine was this: I'd write between five a.m. and eleven, take a cab to the studio, read what I had written to the dancers, then Siobhan would start making movement.

When I asked her what the dance was to be about, she said "Oh, I don't know, something about love and memory and walking."

Some days the composer came and watched. I recorded my poems at his studio and he wove my spoken words throughout the music he began to write. Day by day we each made our small offerings: Jean Marc's sparse electronic score peeled from poems and marine mammal sounds that Brendan sent from the Arctic; my words unwound from the dancers' bodies and Siobhan's stark, sensual movement phrases changed with the shifting wind direction of my words. She said she wanted the dancers to be carried by movement and also driven by it; to show how memories are weighted differently, how time is changed, how some memories leave shadows.

The performance opened in London at Queen Elizabeth Hall, part of the modern South Bank theatre complex across the river from Big Ben. It is an open stage, no proscenium, and David Buckland's stunning sets were 60-foot cloths painted blue with the elongated body of a woman under ice, line drawings of figures in the Inuit style, and the shadows of bodies on the floor. Peter Mumford's lighting reproduced the circling sun, the constant play of light and shadow on ice.

This small book, graced with David Buckland's Arctic images, is part of a greater whole. It is like ice that has broken from the polar cap and drifts free. May you find our small offering to your liking.

—GRETEL EHRLICH

A NOTE ABOUT THE ARTIST

DAVID BUCKLAND has been painting and making photographic images since 1967. His work has been exhibited at the Metropolitan Museum of Art, New York, the Centre Pompidou, Paris, and the National Portrait Gallery, London. His set designs for the Siobhan Davies Dance Company are part of a long association with "Sue," as she is known, and the London dance world.

The making of the sets for *Arctic Heart* was part of a four-way collaboration between Sue, Jean Marc, the composer, and the author. He came to rehearsals almost daily, watched the movement unfold, listened to each new poem and the music into which the spoken text was intertwined, thumbed through books of Inuit art and soon began drawing.

David conceived of the stage as a single ice blue biosphere: vast, cold, seamless. In August 1991 a month before opening night in London, he unrolled two 60-foot long canvas cloths—one to cover the floor of the stage and the other to function as backdrop—and painted them both pale blue.

On the ground cloth that would be stretched taut and tacked to the floor of the stage, appeared ghostly forms—shadows of dancers and ancient images of Inuit seal hunters, the skeletal remains of marine mammals, as well as human footprints on ice.

David explained: "The shadows come from the dancers lying on the floor. It is a history of where they have been, their movement through time and space and the entanglement of desire. They are burned-in marks like the Turin shroud, death shawls in which animals and humans are wrapped as our spirits are ascending.

"On the other hand, the figurative Inuit images are about the spiritual relationship those people maintain with ice, light, cold, darkness, and animals. The simplicity of the images implies the continuum that exists in modern Inuit lives."

On the huge backdrop, David painted a woman's elongated body floating under transparent ice. She dominates the stage with her ethereal, unearthly presence, and all around is an empire of blue and revolving suns whose shadows, like dancers, slide across ice.

—G.E.

RESOLUTE PASSAGE

Between going and coming
heat waves rise from ice;
sun circles us ...
around and around it draws
tight the strings of haloes, seal holes, entrances
to the body of the earth.

Wind blows not
in straight lines but from within: circles
dissolving cycles.

There is no moon, no
night, no water,
only your unexpected heat.

During a three-day storm we
melt winter down in a tin pot.
How much refilling must be done!
Is there no end to
what is white inside us?

Between coming and going
is more coming and going.
Space contorts me.
Wind drives into elbows, armbones ...
guide my hand ...

ONE

I climb ladders of water
and come down as
shattering glass.

I climb ladders of bodies
and come down as
waterless rain.

You are leaves that shake
but what am I?
The sudden collapse of night
after trees have been cut down?

Between endings and beginnings
an arm stirs earth
into sky. Cloud hands,
mountains moving like rivers.
Mountains are clouds.
Bodies move like mountains.
Mountains are water always.

TWO

I look for the tree within,
for the "palm at the end of the mind" whose
trunk is made of woven hair parted
and reparted by wind.

I look for heartwood,
for rings of time,
I look under and over memory because
memory is a solid thing.

Where I was last week, day
does not alternate with night, time
does not come sequenced
but is of a piece: all light with
sun making circles at the horizon,
or else, all darkness
with the moon dragging its forms
across ice.

THREE

Walking is an ambulation of mind; to walk is
to unbalance oneself: I thrust one foot forward
until I almost fall, then the other foot catches me
as if I were two or none or maybe many.

Who teaches a river to walk?
Do mountains lie down?
Is a bird disappointed with air?
Why don't bones go through the skin of the sky?

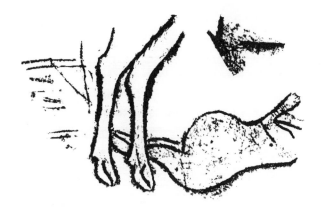

FOUR

I am divided. You left me in half.
You halve me, have had me, have lost me.

And so I go out to see what I can see.

I sleep and when I wake
I am living on Arctic ice 1000 miles
south of the North Pole.
The first day three eider ducks fly by, fly low,
sewing clouds together to be
my second skin.

Everything lives, everything has a voice.
I lie on caribou skin with a man.
The skin caresses us, talks to us.
Threads of silver light fall hard on each horizon;
rocky islands are gray above sheltered inlets:
Resolute Passage, Allen Bay.

A storm circles low
coming from the north, then swinging east, southeast.
For days we live inside its shaking hands.

Everything talks: the walls of the tent and
the wind that talks to walls.
Caribou tells me about ring seals who swim under us:
how sometimes one will climb into a breathing hole
and become a human child.

Everything dead talks about everything living and
everything living billows inward talking to the dead in
voices that sound hollow.

Between tents a three-foot wide crack of ice appears.
The Arctic sea goes down 500 feet.
One day I stumble. My leg goes in, swims away,
and in the morning, grows back again.

Brendan cuts a large hole in the ice so
seals can visit us in the night.
From my bed I peer down
into empires of turquoise,
past walls of white to where ice ends and
blue becomes liquid darkness, and I tell him:
This is the eye into the universe
that has gone past its own seeing.

The skins in the room are alive: his caribou skin moccasins;
the whale's jawbone resting against a house in the village
talks ceaselessly, and polar bear skins
walk at night on ice stained red from where they have feasted on seals.

Can there be too much breathing?
During the storm we clock wind at 45, 50, 65 knots.
Snow drives against the rhinestones of rough ice,
beveling edges, polishing stories told how many times? And farther out,
between grounded floes of ice,
frozen ocean melts into cerulean ponds that walk
all over the place, longing to be one
with the ocean again,

fresh water
merging with salt.

FIVE

Ice is our bed.
You brush my face with wind
you brush my bones.

Sea is the child of ice under us, stirring.
Where ice has melted
the dark reflection of water on clouds
is called water-sky.
It means seals will gather in that place.
It means food and good fortune.

All the blue in the world is here

your eyes
your body diffusing light.

Water walks inside me
I look and see how blue is stirred in.

North of here a chunk of sea ice broke
off and has been floating for years.
People live on it, going where it goes

Now water-sky passes over us
darkening your face my face
the room of air in which our bodies move.

In a dream seals fall out of clouds like snow and
water rises up so that ocean and atmosphere
are one column in which our lives are stacked.

Between coming and going
a mirage appears: the cliffs of distant islands
rise up like walls.
Ice islands float from me like
leaves. Tyndall scattering divides up
the way you see me
until blue drains from the floor of the world
and your eyes guide me through storms

and we lie on wind again
and walk on water.

SIX

Light is a knife that cuts the edge of the polar continent.
Where the shelf breaks off, what begins?

Is ice a mirror?
I walk.

Light is a wall laid under me.
I see you.

Snow drifts in long
rivers flowing from blocks of ice,

the rivers drain:
the floor of the world is blue.

Ice is an eye.
Eye is a heart.

It sees that the body does not lie.
It knows things.

One day is six months long,
followed by one night.

Time takes two steps;
light takes

none at all.

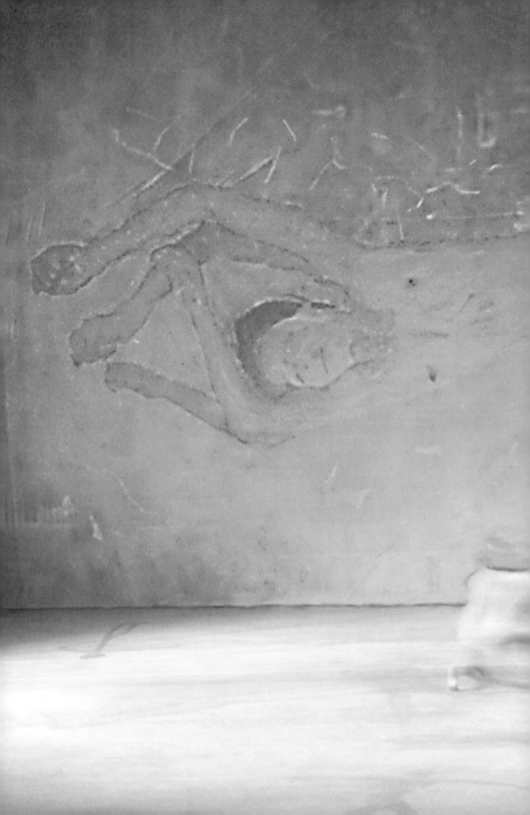

SEVEN

Walking ... I remember stars
I remember moon
I remember night ...walking.
Instead of plants, light rises.
The body is heavy, flowering, turning upward
from winter
like an auger coming out of ice.

Light turns me, separating planes.
How does the body shift to light?

I walk out of light into light,
but I remember night, moon, stars ...
the Big Dipper's handle lifting ... the spread of darkness.
Now ice turns in me.
It walks.
It remembers stars, is made of the mineral of stars.

In autumn ice thickens ...thick as alluvial dirt.
And under it, the sea is black as sky.
I walk.
I look into the lens of
ice for stars.

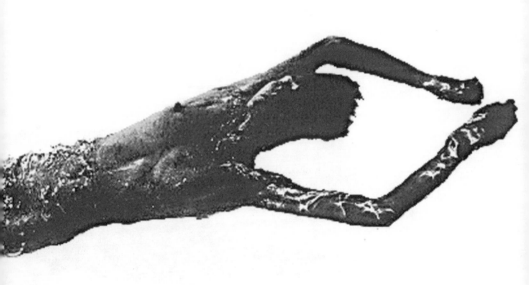

EIGHT

What the wind writes:
the scrawl of a life.

You wrap around my neck and squeeze:
Winter comes undone.
We swim hard inside frozen seas.

Ice is scarred movement.
Ice carves us.

You have led me, dragged me, lifted me;
time twists in my throat.
Where there should be words there is ice.

Fire breaks out in my hands.
Snow mutates. Flying ice skates
the tent slits my skin cuts
sun from the sky.

The heart cracks.
Ice freezes and refreezes.
The top of the world bears scars.

When the ice begins to melt, blue
pools inside us.
Long channels of ice crack open.
Our legs don't hold, don't hold.

Where we stood yesterday on frozen seas a ship
passes demolishing
the place where
our tent was staked to ice.

Bones break – every one of them –
inside you inside me ... they

break open into light
so we can see.

NINE

Stream of light unfolds
in this tent stream
of thought too
narrow for hips too wide
for these windows

Circling sun letting itself
down on us where
words and legs lock
on caribou skins

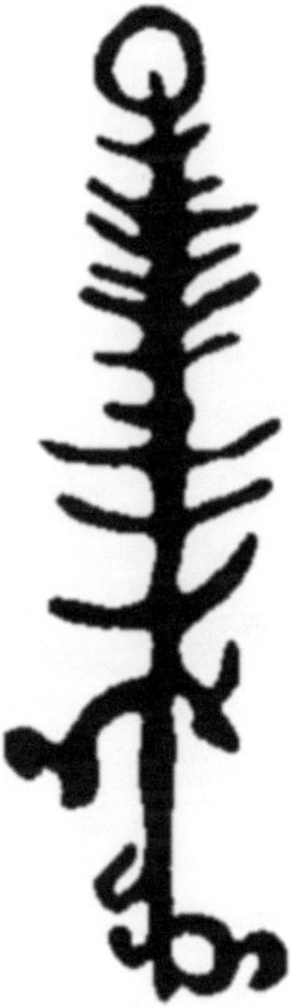

Light cuts us
black dogs stretch us apart
dreams are wedged from sleep:
solitude is recreated. You hum:
Tent flap noise does all the speaking

For days we are laid out
like the dead in a necklace of sun,
my hand on your chest

only seals are breathing

White ravens pick what
shines in your eyes and drink
consciousness

I put my mouth
to your chest:
tent panels bulge

we are living in someone else's lung.

TEN

Day that is night below all this –
I remember now –
it is darkness, heat,
the domestic violence of green

it is where the brain of
ice falls as sweat down foreheads
and loosened hair
is rain.

Down there trees
leaf out and leaves are waves
of birds surging north.

I hear the weekly
plane come and go,
its drone the disappointment
of gravity.

ELEVEN

Ice is time
time is light
light is the passage
the smooth body takes
between these islands
where no moon travels
in spring

Ice is light
light is the time it takes
to leap from winter's
black sky where moon is the only peephole
into this blank of brightness

Time is ice
thickening so deep you
cannot dig to water
then it is water rising
above your waist ...
rising

Ice plus time equals
spring breakup
time plus light equals
December's black

Is life a matter of pigments only?

Light plus light produces no form no shadow
the same as black plus black

Yet we are here.

TWELVE

You walk inside yourself
on roads and ropes
of blood vessels and tendons,

you walk inside yourself
and eat weather
wearing polar bear pants and
river otter shirts the color
of your hair.

You walk inside yourself
and swallow birds' nests,
arctic terns and gulls.

You swallow storms that
sprout on valves and cartilage.

In the afternoon the sky darkens
and rain made of iron splinters deluges
your limbs:
  why are you
  walking alone when you
  can't see the way?

The sea opens up – another
kind of swallowing –
the kayaks laden with ghosts drift by,
ghosts that have taken on
the molted flesh and fur of seals.

Here on this ephemeral ice
where you have broadcast
seed and germinated,

you walk inside yourself
and a whirlwind spins
the story of a body:
  how it is made,
  how it is unmade,
  how love comes into being.

It spins tissue and genes and
desire in magnetic storms on the sun until

you have walked everywhere,
seen everything,

and what is inside us is eaten,
even the calm in the
whirlwind's heart,
even the legs.

This first edition was printed for
Capra Press in September 1992
by McNaughton & Gunn
Ann Arbor, Michigan.

Typography by Denise Eltinge, Santa Barbara

Centerspread: stage performance of *Arctic Heart*
by Siobhan Davies Dance Company, London, 1991.